POETS' WALK

Conversations During the Night

Richard Nelson

I0139936

BROADWAY PLAY PUBLISHING INC
New York
www.broadwayplaypub.com
info@broadwayplaypub.com

POETS' WALK
© Copyright 2022 Richard Nelson

Cover photo: Observation Building in Poets' Walk Park—Red Hook, NY, by Tom Romeo

First edition: October 2022
I S B N: 978-0-88145-953-1

Book design: Marie Donovan
Page make-up: Adobe InDesign
Typeface: Palatino

'Poets' Walk' is the name of a park, or rather a series of trails that skirt along the Hudson River near my home in Rhinebeck, New York. Legend has it that Washington Irving got his idea for *Rip Van Winkle* while walking through this property and gazing out at the Catskill Mountains. Other writers through the ages supposedly have found solace here. It is a place of profound beauty, and, when not crowded on weekends, of peace; here one can lose oneself, or gain a distance from the outside worlds swirling around. It is a place to think.

I have had the good fortune of being a playwright now for nearly fifty years; and during these decades I have had the even greater good fortune of 'placing' my plays in theaters around the country and around the world. In all that time, every single play I have written, and completed to my satisfaction, has found a production; whether in a large Broadway theater, or, as in the midst of the Covid Pandemic, in a seventy-eight-seat space on a college campus. That is, every play except one; the play you have in your hands.

I have shown this play to numerous theaters, friends, colleagues and have received nearly the identical response: an interesting, moving play about loss; however, a play that cannot or will not be produced in America for the foreseeable future. Why? Not because of its content, or opinions expressed, or unmanageable cast size or production requirements. The play, after all, has two characters, and needs only a couple of chairs and a table. The reason is—the two characters in the play, two women in their fifties, one an economics professor, the other an actress, one the widow of a major poet, and the other the poet's sister—these women are Black, and I am a white writer.

When I began to receive this response, I suggested the play be paired with a play by a Black playwright that centered on white characters. My play is pretty short, about sixty-five minutes long so that would not be impossible. And of course there have been many interesting white characters written by Black writers. However, I could find no takers for this idea. So I have decided to publish the play, unproduced.

This play is subtitled 'Conversations During the Night.' And that pretty much sums up its story—two women, closely connected, talk through a night—they share their loss, their confusions about themselves, their worlds, their lives; they do not argue, they make no points, they don't try and convince each other (or the audience) of anything; they are simply complex human beings trying, and mostly struggling, to understand their lives and their world. So—like most of us. At least, that is what I am trying to convey.

In researching the play, I kept a notebook of quotes I found either intriguing or thought provoking. Here is one by Nadine Gordimer, quoted in her obituary: "There are things that Blacks know about whites that we don't know about ourselves. That we conceal and don't reveal in our relationships—and the other way around."

R.N.

CHARACTERS & SETTING

NINA, *50s, an assistant professor of economics at the college. And widow of Samuel, a renowned poet and professor.*

PAULA, *50s, an actress, Samuel's sister and* NINA*'s sister-in-law.*

NINA *and* PAULA *are Black.*

Mentioned, but not in the play:

Gretta, 40s, PAULA*'s partner, an actress.*

Samuel, 50s, PAULA*'s brother and* NINA*'s husband; poet and professor at the college. Recently deceased.*

Henry, NINA *and Samuel's son. Early 20s.*

NINA *and Samuel's home. The kitchen.*

Barrytown, New York. A tiny village on the Hudson River, near the college.

May.

AUTHOR'S NOTE

I use a single quotation mark to notate when the character is paraphrasing, and double quotation marks when the character is actually reading from a source.

"…with each passing day, the words that I hear spoken strike me as less and less descriptive of what things really are."
Philip Roth, *The Human Stain*

"Don't be afraid of race."
Derek Walcott, in an interview

"Father died exactly a year ago, to this very day, the fifth of May, on your name day, Irina…I thought I wouldn't survive."
Anton Chekhov, *Three Sisters*

to Roger and Derek

1.
DO YOU WANT COMPANY?

(Kitchen)

(Sink. Stove. Table. Chairs)

(The middle of the night)

(NINA, in her night clothes, sits at the table with a book. Coffee mug on the table. Other books on the table.)

(Train whistle very close)

(Then:)

(PAULA in nightclothes enters.)

(Hearing the train whistle, NINA looks at her watch, and is startled to see PAULA:)

NINA: *(Startled)* You scared me…

PAULA: Sorry… *(Then)* You're not going to sleep? *(Then)* Trains go by at this time of night?

NINA: It must have been held up, I guess… It's from Montreal. Probably got stuck at the border. That happens a lot… Poor people stuck on the train… *(Then, still looking at her watch:)* You know, Sammy died a year ago, right now… This time… Funny—the train whistle got me to look at my watch right now. Otherwise it would have passed. Exactly now… Give or take… It was confusing at the time.

PAULA: I'm sure…

(Then)

NINA: I have a friend, she told me that once she was waiting on the platform in Rhinecliff—. The man who works there, at the ticket counter, he was also on the platform, and she happened to ask him 'Sir, what's the time?' And he says— 'honey, I threw away my watch the day I joined Amtrak.' *(Smiles)* She loved it that he called her 'honey'.

PAULA: You know coffee doesn't help you sleep.

NINA: What does help?

(Pause)

PAULA: What are you reading?

NINA: Sammy always kept this on the bedside table. Here… *(Reads)* "For a long time I would go to bed early. Sometimes, the candle barely out, my eyes closed so quickly that I did not have time to tell myself, 'I'm falling asleep.' And half an hour later the thought that it was time to look for sleep would awaken me…." He said if Proust can't get us to sleep, then nothing will… *(Looks at* PAULA*)* Doesn't work. Didn't work.

(Pause)

PAULA: *(As she sits)* Happy birthday…

NINA: Thank you. And thank you both for coming. And I'm very happy to finally meet Gretta… She seems really nice… Very very nice. She seems great…

PAULA: I think so. She is. She's sweet. I'm lucky.

NINA: She's asleep?

PAULA: I hope so… I tried to be quiet. *(Then)* So—you want company?

(Lights fade.)

2.
THE NEED TO TALK

(The same. A short time later)

(PAULA is getting herself a glass of water. NINA is still at the table.)

PAULA: When does Henry get here…?

NINA: Tonight sometime.

PAULA: You going to get some sleep before then? Take a nap?

(NINA ignores the question.)

NINA: He's bringing *his* girlfriend.

PAULA: Good. I like her.

(Then)

NINA: You know she cooks.

PAULA: She's a chef, Nina. An assistant chef—in a very good—hard to get into—East Village restaurant. Gretta and I went there… It's very nice. Henry got us in…

NINA: Probably she did. Henry keeps saying what a great cook she is…I wasn't that bad of a cook…

PAULA: I doubt if that was what he meant—.

NINA: *(Over this)* 'Mom, she makes things I've never even heard of.' *(Shrugs)* 'Mom, do you know what *al dente* means?' *(Then)* When he was last here, he made a sandwich and when he cut the bread, he cut it diagonally. We never did. That's not the way he grew up cutting his bread…

(PAULA just looks at NINA.)

(NINA smiles and shrugs again.)

NINA: I know she's going to make me a cake. I'm sure of that.

PAULA: Isn't that a nice thing for her to do?

NINA: It's going to be too much, Paula. Too fancy… Too much… Whatever. I'm not going to like it. But I'll eat it. *(Then)* But I like *her*… You have to… *(Changing the subject)* Let me show you something… *(Picks up a book—a photo album.)* You never met…

PAULA: What?

NINA: Here… *(Points)* Her…

(PAULA looks at a photo.)

PAULA: You had a dog?

NINA: She was Sammy's. He got her after Henry went off to college. He needed a friend I think. That's what I think anyway…

(Smiles)

PAULA: Very cute.

NINA: And all these years I thought he didn't like dogs. When I wanted a dog… And she'd just follow Sammy around… It was pathetic. *(Laughs to herself)* You want to know her name? The dog?

PAULA: What was her name?

NINA: It's a story… *(The story)* We're in Philly, visiting his Mom, one of those million visits when she was ill.

PAULA: I went too…

NINA: And we're walking down, I think, Lombard, maybe not, say it's Lombard—anyway near his Mom's, and Sammy and I, we walk past this man walking his dog. It's a little white dog… *(Points to the picture)* …and he, this man, is a very large, huge, handsome, Black man. And as we walk by, we hear him say—to his dog,

'Come on, Whitey. Come on, hurry up. Don't take all day, Whitey…' *(Smiles)* So—*he* now had to get a dog.

PAULA: Of course.

NINA: *(Pointing out in the photo)* Whitey… *(She looks at the photo.)* Sammy'd walk Whitey through the campus… This tall dignified Black man, esteemed writer, poet, with this little white fluffy—*his* dog—*she*—was very fluffy— 'Whitey'. *(In Sammy's voice)* 'Hey, Whitey… Come on.' Always a loud voice… He had such a deep loud voice. Resonant.

PAULA: I know.

NINA: And he'd watch the kids turn around and look at him. 'We've waited long enough, Whitey. We've waited a long time. Now hurry up.' *(She takes a last sip of her cold coffee.)* He'd look at the kids and say, 'oh, come on, come on, it's funny…' *(Then)* They were inseparable…

(Then)

PAULA: That is funny… Very Sammy… *(She turns a page, stops at another photo.)*

NINA: *(Explains the photo)* His fiftieth. So a while ago. The poetry press a couple doors down the street. There's a poetry press… They had the party.

PAULA: I didn't know there was a—

NINA: A press? Just down the street… Nice people… *(Points out:)* Ashbery.

PAULA: That's him?

NINA: He'd long been retired from the college, but he came down from Hudson for Sammy's party… He liked Sammy's work a lot… Wrote about it.

(PAULA turns a page.)

NINA: Whitey died like one month after Sammy…
The vet said cancer, I think a broken heart. *(Pointing
out another photo)* That's Henry at a friend's house.
Just down the street… It's been fixed up now… It was
funky… *(She looks closely.)* Artsy people… *(Then, as she
looks at the photo:)* There's a real estate woman here—I
think she used to be an actress… *(Nods to* PAULA*)*

PAULA: I have friends who've given up acting to—. In
LA I thought of doing that—.

NINA: She's very aggressive. Or assertive. She leaves
hanging on our door knobs these little—fliers—
'interested in selling your house?' With a photo of an
attractive young woman in heels, swinging her purse,
skirt up over her knee, holding a take-out coffee…
(Then) People don't look like that here… Maybe now…
I don't know. I guess now. *(Another photo:)* Olana.
Henry liked going there… Run down the hill… Looks
like we're in Morocco, not just up 9G. *(Another photo:)*
Edgewater…

PAULA: What's that? That sounds familiar.

NINA: Sammy never took you there? Just at the end of
our little street.

PAULA: He didn't.

NINA: On the water… Old eighteenth century house.
Beautiful. Gore Vidal lived in it for years.

PAULA: Huh…

NINA: When he taught at Bard, Paula. A sweet very
wealthy man then bought it. Fixed it all up. He'd have
picnics just for us from the street… Writers. Politicians
had stayed there… Famous people. Sammy wrote a
poem about it…

PAULA: Ah that's why I know the name…

(Another photo:)

NINA: You and Samuel... How young are you there...?
Pictures are all mixed together.

(PAULA *looks:*)

PAULA: (*Answers the question*) Young...

NINA: I wake up sometimes, and I swear that I hear
him downstairs making me coffee, Paula...

PAULA: (*Hesitates then*) Who?

NINA: (*Obviously*) Sammy. I can smell the coffee being
made. Then I come downstairs...

PAULA: And...

NINA: ...and he's not here... Obviously... (*Then*) When
I invited the real estate agent to look at the house.

PAULA: So you're thinking of selling it...

NINA: You wake up and think lots of things. She
wandered around, in and out of rooms, took notes.
Then wrote down a price...I have it... (*Stands and
goes and gets a piece of paper out of her purse as:*) 'We'll
start here...' she said. I mean just to pack up Sammy's
stuff—the books, boxes of... —it's like a mountain in
front of you.

PAULA: I'm sure. My brother never threw anything
away.

(NINA *looks at the piece of paper:*)

NINA: You want to know the price?

(PAULA *looks at* NINA,)

(*Then:*)

PAULA: No.

NINA: Good answer... (*She puts the piece of paper
away.*) I've put together a box of stuff for you... Some
things he actually said— 'this stuff should go to my
sister'. He'd organized some things. I made him. Not

everything. He has a superstition—had—about talking too much about it…

PAULA: A lot of people do. It's pretty common I think.

NINA: Is it? So maybe while you're here you can go through the box…

PAULA: Sure. I'm curious about what my brother wanted me to have.

NINA: It took me a whole afternoon to find everything he'd… you know…

PAULA: I understand…

NINA: You keep getting caught up… Can you take things back..?

PAULA: To the city? Yes. We have the car…

NINA: You want any breakfast?

PAULA: It's the middle of the night.

NINA: There's cereal and… That's it. I don't think I have any eggs. I don't have much of anything else…

(Another photo:)

PAULA: How old is Henry here?

NINA: Let me see… I think about fourteen….

(Lights fade)

3.
QUESTIONS

(The same. A short time later)

(NINA is making herself a bowl of cereal—cutting up a banana, etc. Paula sits at the table.)

PAULA: He could get me so angry, Nina. He had those long arms and he'd hold my head and tell me to hit him. I couldn't reach him.

NINA: What are you talking about?

PAULA: When we were kids. *(Obviously)* He was older. He should have treated me…I was half his size…

(NINA *laughs.*)

PAULA: Don't laugh. Once he came home from school, I was thinking about this the other day. And in gym class they were teaching the boys how to wrestle. He wanted to show me what he'd learned. I was flattered he wanted to show me. So we go down to the grungy apartment building basement. All concrete. Spider webs. He says—'you wrestle on a mat.' We didn't have a mat, that why he's brought down from upstairs—a towel. A fucking towel, Nina. This thick [very thin]. And gets us into position and—bang! That's my head. He throws me on the ground. 'See what I learned today?' he says. So goddamn proud of himself. 'Again…?' he says. Like a challenge now. And you don't challenge me… So—we do it again… He says, 'Now that you know what's coming…', and then—'bang' again. My fucking head. Three times he does this. He stops he says because— *(A voice)* I'm crying…

(Then)

NINA: I never heard that… He never told me that. Maybe he forgot. We all remember different things…

PAULA: Another time?

NINA: Go ahead.

PAULA: At Halloween time—Sammy and I are home, Mom's somewhere—probably working. So just us. Our apartment is right above the front stoop. You've heard this…

NINA: No.

PAULA: So my brother has a 'plan'. That's what he calls it, 'a plan'. He fills a bunch of balloons with water, and tells me to 'guide' his friends, when they show up trick or treating—to a spot on the stoop, right under our window. And then he's going to drop the balloon on them, he says.

(NINA *laughs*.)

PAULA: But each time, Nina, each time he drops a balloon, he misses—and instead the balloons hit me. Each time. I end up soaked. And—crying.

(NINA *smiles and begins to eat her cereal*.)

PAULA: When I cried he stopped… Did he do things like that to you?

NINA: *(Laughs)* No. Not like that… We were adults Paula. *(Then)* He teased…

PAULA: Of course…

NINA: I teased him back.

(Then)

PAULA: You know he taught me to read.

NINA: Sammy? Don't you think you'd have learned to read anyway?

PAULA: Sure. But I still can see his fingers—beautiful hands he had—

NINA: True.

PAULA: —moving along the page—slowly under each word. He'd say the word. Then I would say it… *(Beginning a list)* He taught me to swim…

NINA: I tried to teach him to drive…

PAULA: I didn't think he ever wanted to drive. Like cooking…

NINA: I gave up… It wasn't easy… It wasn't fun… *(Short pause)* He said something to me, a couple of days before he died…

PAULA: What?

NINA: He said, 'to me poetry is an intimate and
domestic thing, Nina'. We were at breakfast— *(Like
here at this table)* —he said he was most interested
in describing how the table looks in the morning...
and there across the table sits his wife [me]; how she
looks... Me... *(Then)* He said... *(She stops.)*

PAULA: What?

NINA: He said he wanted now to convey a casual tone
in his poetry—he said, and I quote him: 'like throwing
a jacket on a chair.' He wanted to write like that...

(Short pause)

PAULA: This I know you don't know. I made Sammy
promise never to tell anyone.

NINA: I'm interested.

PAULA: I was in high school and I wrote a poem and I
showed it to Sammy. He's now a published poet...

NINA: That was courageous of you. *(Smiles)* He could
be tough...

PAULA: *(Shrugs)* He was my brother. Why not? One
part of my poem: *(She recites:)*
"On the Cape, I reach my arm across the sea..."
I remember it... *(Continues)*
"The beach curls across my feet,
My face stretches up to the sky
As from above a cloud breaks wind..."
(She shakes her head.)
'Breaks wind.' I'd never heard the phrase. It's actually
a beautiful phrase—on its own. He was merciless.

NINA: I can imagine...

PAULA: *(Over this)* For days, he'd just look at me, start
to smile and laugh. His horse laugh.

NINA: Actually, he told me that story… *(She continues to eat her cereal.)*

(PAULA will begin to eat as well—a banana, and finally make herself some cereal as well.)

PAULA: I visited my son…

NINA: Already. Good. You told me you wanted to do that.

PAULA: It just happened.

NINA: When?

PAULA: Two weeks ago.

NINA: Good. How was it?

PAULA: Fine…

NINA: How did he treat you?

PAULA: I'm going to try and get back into his life.

NINA: He's okay with that?

PAULA: I don't know. I'm trying. Now that I'm back on the East Coast. *(Then)* He still lives two blocks from his father. They're still very close. I didn't see the father…I didn't take Gretta.

NINA: I understand.

PAULA: My son's a nurse…I didn't know. In a clinic in a poor neighborhood in Brooklyn. He does something valuable. I'm proud of him… *(Smiles)* Puts me to shame…

NINA: It's not a competition, Paula…

PAULA: *(Smiles)* No… He told me he's thinking of changing jobs… He asked me what I thought.

NINA: He wanted your opinion. That's a good sign.

PAULA: Or he was being polite.

NINA: Probably not….

PAULA: What right do I have…? To give advice to him. This is interesting. He's been offered a job at a firm… They have their own clinic. Health service. A tech firm in the West Village. Pays a lot he said.

NINA: Good. If that's what he wants.

PAULA: He said, they need more Black faces…

NINA: They told him that? In those words…

PAULA: I think it's something he figured out… From things being said, not said… But maybe in those words… Pays a lot.

NINA: Right.

PAULA: He asked me, 'Am I considering this because it's something I want or because it's something I can now do?'

NINA: Interesting.

PAULA: 'So should I take advantage of this?' 'Is it going to last?'

NINA: What did you say?

PAULA: I hadn't seen him for ten years, Nina. *(Shrugs)* I want what he wants. I want him to like me…

NINA: Sure… *(Then)* I have friends teaching at colleges… Same thing. I'm told head hunters are going to college websites and especially economics departments and looking for Black faces… And a Black woman…? 'Wow. Oh my God.' 'Jackpot…' 'Check…' 'Checkmark…' Especially banks and hedge funds…

PAULA: They don't reach out to you?

NINA: My friend Elizabeth, she's taking a job at a Wall Street firm. Pays a lot more than teaching here. I recommended her.

PAULA: What do you mean?

NINA: They'd called me up... *(Then)* I think the headhunter goes on line—and looks. Like I said. Hunts. They found me. 'Checkmark.' I thought about it...I made the mistake of telling my son. He says I'm just scared...

PAULA: Are you?

NINA: Of what? What am I scared of, Paula?

PAULA: Of whatever your son thinks you're scared of...

NINA: No, I'm not scared. I said to them 'I know what you're looking for.' So I told them about Elizabeth... 'Economics Department, Vassar'. That did it. 'Go look her up...' And they did... And she fit the bill. I knew that... 'Jackpot...'

(Short pause)

PAULA: Is that why you were thinking of selling the house?

NINA: When—?

PAULA: The real estate agent... Coming here. So you thought about this...

NINA: I guess I did. For a little while... *(Then)* I think I might have been interested—if they'd just been looking for an academic economist. Only that...I'm a very good economist...

PAULA: Right...I see.

NINA: But they want something else. And that's not what I'm willing to sell... *(Short pause)* We were talking about your son...

PAULA: Right. Gretta asked me if I now regret having given him up...

NINA: She asks tough questions... *(Smiles)* What'd you say?

(No response)

PAULA: She asked me if I had tried to abort him...

NINA: She guessed?

PAULA: I suppose. *(She nods.)* She's got me doing an audition tape. For her agent... She said, if I'm moving from LA, then I should do more than just stupid commercials.

NINA: Don't they pay—?

PAULA: She's pushing me... And that's good, I think. She even picked out the speech for...

NINA: The audition...

PAULA: I think I will have some cereal... *(Then, as she gets her cereal she recites:)* Here. See if you know it...I didn't.
"Grief fills the room up of my absent child,
Lies in his bed, walks up and down with me,
Puts on his pretty looks, repeats his words,
Remembers me of all his gracious parts,
Stuffs out his vacant garments with his form.
Then have I reason to be fond of grief.
Fare you well. Had you such a loss as I,
I could give better comfort than you do.
I will not keep this form upon my head,
When there is such disorder in my wit.
Oh Lord! My boy, my Arthur, my fair son!
My life, my joy, my food, my all the world!
My widow-comfort, and my sorrows' cure!"

(Then)

NINA: Shakespeare?

PAULA: Yeh. She said she thought I could 'bring something of myself to this.' Her words. I said I can't do Shakespeare... From a play I'd never read. Never even heard of...Gretta said he wrote this soon after his own son had died... So... *(Then)* So, as I said, she's pushing me… *(Then)* I remembered something Sammy said…

NINA: What?

PAULA: How a poem, any art, how that can solve nothing. It actually does nothing. It doesn't heal. It doesn't forgive. I doesn't forget. It's just a companion. Or a friend. Someone to share things with… And that's important too…

(Then)

NINA: *(About the cereal)* You have what you need?

PAULA: I'm good.

NINA: I like Gretta.

PAULA: I'm lucky…

(Then)

NINA: I was going through Sammy's books, Paula…

PAULA: That's a job. Why that look?

NINA: I wanted to keep them together. Maybe a library would want them… I made some calls. One said they'd come and choose. I asked if they'll only pick the 'good stuff?' *(Then)* This I need to talk to you about… There was an interesting book I'd never seen before. A novel. I don't know why it caught my eye, except it was on a special shelf, where he had books by friends. It was inscribed to him… A very warm inscription. 'Joyce.' I read the book… *(Then)* About two friends, a young man and older woman. They spend time together. Are really compatible. He's a writer. She has money and helps him meet people. Important people in publishing. The writer gets a book published and coming back from a book signing, in a taxi—he kisses her, and that changes their relationship. He is confused—he's married. And breaks things off. Then he regrets it. Reaches out to her, but now she's getting

married to someone else. Who he says is boring… And
this story ends the story with what a boring life the
young man now will have… *(Then)* In Samuel's first
story… The first he published. In *The New Yorker.* He
rarely wrote prose.

PAULA: I know. Looked down on it.

NINA: But he wrote a story and published it… About
a young man and an older woman… Friends. She
helps him out in some way. In a taxi *she* kisses *him*…
That changes the relationship. They separate—but
not before going to bed a few times… And then in
Sammy's story, *she* gets married to a boring man and
she will have a boring life… *(She looks at* PAULA.*)* This
was published in the magazine a few months after her
book came out. I checked when her book came out.
(Then) Were they talking to each other here? Through
their writing? This 'Joyce' and my Sammy?

(No response)

NINA: Do you know anything about this, Paula?

PAULA: About what?

NINA: Such a woman. 'Joyce.'

PAULA: No.

NINA: Would you tell me if you did?

(No response)

NINA: Texas is buying his papers. They're sending
someone… So I've been going through everything first.
That's my reason for…I'm not just…

PAULA: What?

(Smiles)

NINA: I'm not. And it takes forever. You get stopped
reading… There's a poem, almost an epic, pages and
pages long. He never published it. And, very unlike

him, it's about a real person. The actor, singer, Paul Robeson.

PAULA: I remember when he was interested in Robeson. I even loaned him some stuff that I had…

NINA: Did you? The Robeson I know about was very political…

PAULA: I know that.

NINA: *(Over this)* But this poem is about before that. When he just wanted to be an actor, Nina. That's all he wanted. In the twenties, and he's doing **Othello** in London. Sammy really catches that feeling in the verse. With the rhythms. The nineteen twenties…

PAULA: I'd like to see that…

NINA: I'll show it to you… *(Continues)* Robeson, in the poem—and I believe in life too now that I've done my own reading –. He also had books. Robeson meets a young white sometime actress… And falls for her. Head over heels in love. Passionate verse. Sensual. Sexual. Sammy at his very best… Like his early stuff…

PAULA: I know…

(Then)

NINA: In the poem, Robeson's Black friends—and there are a few in London at the time—to them, she's 'something of a slut.' That's a line of the poem. And to Robeson's wife—he has a wife, she also is his business manager—there's this line, in quotes, so I'm guessing he pulled it from a letter or somewhere. Research he did. I don't know. Actually the wife's more like a sister to him now, it seems… In the poem. That's the feeling. *(Then)* When she finds a love letter to this woman, Yolanda, is the white woman's name, the wife says—

PAULA: In the poem.

NINA: Yeh. She says: 'you are just one more Negro musician pursing white meat.' *(Then)* There's a comical section when he actually visits Yolanda's house and family...Sammy makes them into cartoon figures. The wife complains that Yolanda is 'exhausting' him... *(Then)* Yolanda is pressured by her family and her friends to break off the affair. Because he's Black? It isn't said. But she succumbs. And Robeson has a speech where he calls her 'a free spirit, bright, loving, wonderful woman.' And 'the great love of my life...' *(Then)* And then Robeson in the poem tries and fails to kill himself—over this woman.

PAULA: Is that true?

(NINA shrugs.)

NINA: It's a poem. *(She looks at PAULA.)* One canto, that's what Sammy calls them—is farcical, or maybe not. Actually sort of bittersweet. You know who was his wife's closest friend during all this time? In London? You'll never guess. The playwright Noel Coward. Incredible. This young Black woman hanging out with this gay white guy. In Sammy's poem he makes her laugh. That reminded me of you and your gay male friends way back... Remember how they made me laugh...? *(Then)* I kept telling myself as I was reading this long poem... It is just a poem about Paul Robeson...

(Lights fade.)

4.
PAUL ROBESON

(Same)

(Short time later)

(NINA has put on a CD in the CD player:)

(AN old scratched recording of Paul Robeson singing Curly Headed Baby:)
Oh, my baby, my curly-headed baby,
We'll sit below the sky and sing a song
To the moo-oo-oo-oon.

PAULA: You know that's my CD. I loaned it to Sammy when I guess he was researching Robeson… For that poem.

NINA: You're right. It does have your initials… Looks like Sammy tried to rub them off… *(She laughs to herself.)* I hadn't noticed that. I'll put it in your box of stuff…
Oh, my baby, my little darkie baby,
Your daddy's in the cotton field,
Workin' for the fo-oo-oo-oo-od
We're not going to wake up Gretta are we?

PAULA: She's a sound sleeper…

NINA: Don't tell me about it…
So, la-la-la-la-la-la lullaby-by.
Does you want the moon to play with?
All the stars to run away with?
They'll come if you you don't cry.
So, la-la-la-la-la-la lullaby-by.
Sammy used to sing this to Henry…I wonder if he remembers…

PAULA: Play it for him and see…

NINA: Maybe I will… I put it on after I read the poem…

PAULA: Our Mom sang this to us. To me at least…

NINA: With a deep voice?

PAULA: She couldn't do that.

NINA: Sammy sang it that way…

PAULA: I'll bet…
In the mammy's arms be creepin',

An' soon you'll be a-sleepin'.
Laa-laa la-la-la-la-la lullaby
Oh, my baby, my curly-headed baby,
I'll dance you fast asleep and love you so
As I si-ii-ii-ii-ing
Oh, my baby, my little darkie baby,
Jus' tuck your head like little bird,
Below its mammy's wi-ii-ii-ii-ing
So, la-la-la-la-la-la lullaby-by
Do you want the moon to play with?
All the stars to run away with?
They'll come if you you don't cry.
So, la-la-la-la-la-la lullaby-by.
In the mammy's arms be creepin',
An' soon you'll be a-sleepin'.
Laa-laa la-la-la-la-la-la lullaby
(Song finishes)

(Short pause)

NINA: And he sang it to your Mom… When she
was so ill. Now I see—she must have sung it to him
too… *(Then)* Your mom told us a story about your
grandma… Sammy said he'd never heard this. When
Mom was very ill… *(She looks at* PAULA.*)* I call her
'Mom…'

PAULA: What story?

NINA: Your grandma, it seems, was a lot younger than
your grandpa…

PAULA: I don't know.

NINA: In fact, he was closer to her mother's age. Your
great grandma's age. Who—was also in love with him.
Your great grandma was in love with her daughter's,
your grandma's, husband.

PAULA: I've never heard this.

NINA: And she said, this was not a secret. Your
grandpa, anytime he bought a present for his wife,
he had to buy one for his mother-in-law too. She—
also turned up at the hotel of the couple on their
honeymoon…

PAULA: No.

NINA: You're right, I don't know if it's true. Too good
to be true… Sammy too thought she'd made it up…
Or heard it about someone else. She liked to make up
stories…

PAULA: (Nods) Sammy said that's where he got his 'gift'
from…

NINA: Right. Sammy called this his mother's art…
It reminded him of something he'd read, he didn't
remember where: 'art is what makes life more
interesting than art…' He kept that on a card on his
desk. (Then) I should send you a poem of his. He
never published it either. It wasn't for that. When your
Mom was dying… It wasn't really a poem, more of a
puzzle to keep thinking about something else besides
her dying. The first letter of each line, read down the
page—her name in full. The last letter of each line—
'The quality of mercy…'

PAULA: What she was always… She was always
quoting that to us…

NINA: That's what Sammy said…

PAULA: Growing up….

NINA: He'd work on it on the train, going down to
Philly. And on the way back… 'Some place,' he said,
'where he could lose himself.' Once we got there and
she wasn't in her room. And Sammy—I'd never seen
him like this… Like a wave of sound came out of his
mouth 'where is she?' (Then) Farrar keeps asking for
what he'd left…I'm not going to give them that….

PAULA: What about the Robeson poem?

(NINA *ignores that.*)

(NINA *puts on another Robeson song; My Lindy Lou.*)
Lindy, did you hear that mockingbird sing last night?
Honey, he was singin' so sweet in the moonlight
In the old magnolia tree
Bustin' his heart with melody
I know he was singin' of you
Mah Lindy Lou
Lindy Lou
I'd lay right down and die and die
If I could sing like that bird sings to you

NINA: We danced to this…. Sammy'd go down on his
knee… He was a clown…

PAULA: Always was…

(NINA *starts to dance.*)

(PAULA *joins, and they will dance together as:*)

Mah little Lindy Lou
Lindy, did you smell that honeysuckle
Honey, he was smellin' so sweet in the moonlight
Clingin' round my cabin door
Reckon it's 'cause he loves you so
Honey, that's the way I love you
Mah Lindy Lou
Lindy Lou
I'd lay right down and die and die
If I could be as sweet as that to you
Mah little Lindy Lou…

(*Lights fade.*)

5.
A GREAT BLACK POET.

(The same)

(A short time later.)

(As NINA *and* PAULA *both eat their cereal:)*

NINA: "I'm not a Black poet. I don't think of myself that way."

PAULA: I can hear Sammy saying that.

NINA: Me too.

PAULA: Who was this student?

NINA: One of Sammy's… He just graduated. It was at the graduation last week that he told me this. He found me at the picnic, he said, 'Professor, do you have a moment…' I said of course.

PAULA: He's Black.

NINA: Yeh… He had Sammy for a literature class as a Sophomore. He said one day, when he was confused, he visited Sammy's office, and that's what Sammy said, how he doesn't—didn't—see himself that way… This young man told him he'd been at some group, a club, maybe it was a class, I don't know. And the students all met in a circle. A group from different colleges, I think. *(Then)* And he's one of two Black students there. The students being asked their ambitions and their backgrounds, and they've been asked—where do you see yourselves in, I think, five years? *(Then)* He said the other Black student, she started talking about what it's like being Black… And then how everyone, he said, got really quiet, very very polite. Everyone 'listened' in quotes. His words. No one asked her anything. Didn't question. Didn't add anything of their own. And when this student had finished, this young man could see that the other students expected him now to talk.

About, he assumed—being Black. He said, he guessed
'as an expert'. He found that uncomfortable. And
confusing... And so he found his way to Sammy...
(Then) He wanted me to know that... He'd been
meaning to write me ever since Sammy died... He said
he'd tried two or three times...

(Short pause)

PAULA: Did he say something...to that group?

NINA: I asked him that. He didn't. But—it had crossed
his mind, he said—and this so reminded me of Samuel,
that wicked sense of humor—to say something so
outrageous, because he knew no one would dare
question whatever the hell he said...

PAULA: I've been in situations like that.

NINA: I'm sure you have.

PAULA: And who can you ever talk about it with?

NINA: Well, it's just us. No one's listening...

PAULA: And I've seen people take advantage of that...

NINA: Tell me about it. Of course they have... Sammy
had said to him, 'You feel you are more than that,
right?'

(NINA and PAULA eat.)

NINA: I had him over to dinner this week. Before he
left... We sat here...I told him a story Sammy told
me...

PAULA: What story?

NINA: Do you know it?

PAULA: I don't know what you're going to say.

NINA: About a friend of his, a writer, he's asked to
write the dialogue for a musical—about Martin Luther
King. This friend's white, and before he agreed he'd
said to the producers— 'don't you want a Black

writer for this?' But they were in a hurry, they'd fired someone and rehearsals were about to begin and so they convinced Sammy's friend that it would be all right. And he convinced himself because, as he told Sammy, King was his hero too. You don't know this.

PAULA: No.

NINA: The friend writes and writes and then goes to the rehearsals and all seems fine until he's told— that some of the other producers—there are other producers—have concerns—that he's white... *(Then)* So now in the midst of everything, putting on a show, he's asked if he'd take on a co-writer.

PAULA: Someone Black.

NINA: Of course. He says sure, but so they'll get the right person, could he get notes so he'd know where he was going wrong and what to fix. He gets no notes. *(Then)* Then they come back to him and ask—would he accept a co-writer—who he wouldn't have to ever meet. Who wouldn't actually write anything. But the two of them would share the credit... *(Then)* He told them they could go to hell. Fuck off. And quit. *(Short)* Sammy said to me, that he always had his 'radar' up, making sure he wasn't that 'co-writer' in quotes. There to 'smooth' things out for others... He said—we have to be careful.

(Phone rings.)

(As NINA *gets her phone:)*

NINA: The young man was very interested in that story... *(She answers the phone. Into the phone:)* Hi... Yeh. *(To* PAULA*)* Henry... *(Into the phone)* I just wanted to hear your voice...I'm okay...

*(*PAULA *stands.)*

PAULA: *(Mouths and gestures)* Can I make coffee...?

(NINA *nods.*)

NINA: *(Into the phone)* I think my party is at seven…

(NINA *looks to* PAULA *who nods.*)

NINA: It's small. I'm with your Aunt. I will… *(To* PAULA*)* Henry says hi…

PAULA: Hi back… *(She begins to organize making coffee in a coffee maker—clean out the pot, get a filter, etc. as:)*

NINA: *(Into the phone)* Okay. Drive carefully… Say hi to your girlfriend. *(Then)* 'Rebecca…' Right. I remember. Okay. Okay. Love you too… *(She hangs up.)*

PAULA: He calls you at—?

NINA: He knows I don't sleep. And I left a message to call when he could… *(Then)* Now I guess he could… Been busy…

PAULA: He knows you don't sleep?

NINA: You're finding everything? I can—.

PAULA: Sit… I haven't seen Henry in…

NINA: At Sammy's….

PAULA: Right. Of course. That was the last time.

NINA: He sent his love…

PAULA: I heard… *(Then)* Gretta told me a funny story…

NINA: What? We need funny stories…

PAULA: We do… You know she teaches a bit too…

NINA: I didn't know… We just met. I want to get to know her.

PAULA: *(Over this)* One day she drops into a rehearsal of a student play… A Black student's play. Very talented she said. There were three characters all are Black. Three big guys. And in rehearsal room there's also a Black drummer, Black director. And assigned by the teacher to be the stage manager—the one following

the script for the actors—is a very young looking, very
small, very pale, white girl from, she thinks, Nebraska.
Somewhere like that. And this girl's following along in
the script, when one of the actors calls out: 'line'. He's
forgotten his line. It's a rehearsal. The dialogue in this
play is very raw, and almost every other word—is the,
the N-word.

NINA: Right. Is that necessary…?

PAULA: That's not the point. Anyway, so this actor calls
out 'line'. *(Then)* Pause. He looks to the stage manager.
'Line.' *(Then)* The other actors, the director, and even
the drummer all now look to the stage manager. Again
he calls out: 'Line!' Her face is red. 'Line!' shouted now.
'Line!' *(Then)* Then finally she reads the line, which
goes something like, 'Fuck you N-word, N-word,
N-word, fuck you. You fucking 'N-word.' Of course
she can't say 'N-word' she has to say the word. For
a moment, I don't know how long the room is silent.
This small white girl shouting out these words in this
room. When all of sudden all these big guys, they
fall on the floor laughing. *(She laughs.)* Everyone is
laughing. Except for the little stage manager who is
almost crying…

(NINA and PAULA both laugh.)

NINA: Sammy would have loved that story.

PAULA: I know.

NINA: He'd have told it at faculty cocktail parties.
Where he'd always make jokes. They'd just look at
him. I remember him once at one of these parties,
after telling it, he shouts out: 'Come on. Suppose
Aristophanes had had good taste!' *(Then)* Sammy had
a close friend—a biology professor, white—you'll meet
him, he's coming to my birthday party. We'd go out to
eat in Tivoli, and if we got to the restaurant first, when
his friend entered, Sammy would say, pretty loudly,

'here's my honkey...' You have to laugh, he said...
Make fun of it...

(When the coffee is ready, PAULA *will pour herself some and offer* NINA *some as well.)*

NINA: Thank you... You're not going back to bed.

PAULA: No... *(Then)* I was in an acting class. Last week. Again, Gretta...

NINA: She's getting you to do a lot.

PAULA: I need it. I need to be pushed....

NINA: I know...

PAULA: We're rehearsing a scene. And the teacher says, say your line but to a different person, different character...

NINA: Why?

PAULA: Wait... One of my lines is— 'I don't know, maybe I'm just not smart enough to understand.' I'd been saying this as a joke to the character who's my brother. Now I say it to the character who's my mother, it means something totally different. 'Every line,' he said, 'the same words, mean something different when said to different people.'

NINA: I don't understand...

PAULA: His point, Nina: something can have meaning for one person and mean nothing or something, even the opposite to someone else.

NINA: *(A joke)* Your beautiful line: 'breaking wind...'

PAULA: What? I guess. I shouldn't have mentioned that. *(Continues)* He said, that is how I want you to think of your character. How she is different in each relationship. Each conversation. And so how people, human beings—which after all is what we're trying to portray—they, we, are very complicated. *(Then)* So let's not simplify our characters. That only trivializes them. Every time we simplify, we trivialize the human being.

(Then)

NINA: I could have said that to Sammy's student...

PAULA: I know. That's why I thought of it.

(Then)

NINA: At graduation last weekend—they announced a scholarship in Sammy's name.

PAULA: I know... They wrote and asked me for money.

NINA: Did you give—?

PAULA: No. What money do I have...?

NINA: Anyway. There was a big presentation at the awards dinner... A lot of people had given money.

PAULA: Good.

NINA: The person announcing this scholarship—from the Board I think—he wasn't a professor. He didn't know Sammy. He called Samuel—'a Great Black poet'.

(Lights fade.)

6.
POETS' WALK

(The same)

(A short time later)

(NINA and PAULA are going through papers, a few books:)

PAULA: *(With a notecard)* What's this...?

NINA: Read it... *(Explaining)* Sammy was always sending Henry quotations—on postcards, birthday cards... Or just for no reason. Things he wanted to share with his son. Read it... What's on that? Things to help...

PAULA: What do you mean?

NINA: Read…Henry didn't take them with him…I found them in his room…

PAULA: In quotes… *(Reads)* "…the growing good of the world is partly dependent on un-historic acts, and that things are not so ill with you and me as they might have been is half owing to the number who lived faithfully a hidden life and rest in unvisited tombs." From what?

NINA: You don't know it?

PAULA: Tell me. Do you know?

NINA: *Middlemarch.* The very end. Sammy's advice— not to pressure yourself too much, when you're young. How seemingly small things matter… Henry, I think he felt was pressuring himself. Maybe having a famous father. He wanted his son to relax. And that things were not so bad…

PAULA: *Middlemarch?*

NINA: Yeh. What?

PAULA: A Black father sends his Black son a quote from George Elliot?

NINA: *(A real question)* Why not? *(Then)* Henry kept them all… *(The cards)*

PAULA: *(Another)* 'Happy birthday.' *(Reads)* Orwell: "A writer's subject matter will be determined by the age he lives in."

NINA: For a few years Henry wanted to be a poet. So Sammy's giving advice…

PAULA: *(Another)* 'Nothing exterior shall ever take command of me.' That contradicts…

NINA: Exactly. Probably Sammy would say both are true… He wanted to talk Art to his son… You know he felt that was important… *(Then)* I should get a birthday card, it's my birthday…

PAULA: From Sammy?

NINA: Why not? Let me see… *(She takes a few cards.)* A poem…. He told me when he was a young poet, he met Derek Walcott. And it was Walcott who told him to drop the capital letters at the front of every line, use lower-case.

(Shows PAULA*)*

NINA: Sammy said the moment he did that, he felt 'refreshed.' It made him relax.

PAULA: I've told you we Zoomed two days before…

NINA: You told me… *(She continues to look through the cards.)* And you said he looked fine.

PAULA: He was there in his T-shirt. Probably in his underwear. I couldn't tell.

NINA: Probably…

PAULA: He was a little grumpy with me. I'd probably interrupted his writing.

NINA: Could have been anything. *(She sighs.)*

PAULA: What?

NINA: Henry…Sammy told him, it's a really hard life. Just ask your aunt.

PAULA: Being an actor?

*(*NINA *nods.)*

NINA: You haven't heard this. He told him…

PAULA: Henry?

NINA: When you pretend—on stage—meaning when you are acting—you are someone else. Another person… Saying things you wouldn't or couldn't say yourself. But you'll say them out loud in front of

people... To imagine yourself as someone else, with
someone else's feelings, someone else's history...
That's important to be able to do... And that's not a
bad thing to share... It has its worth... *(Then)* And, he
said, that is very much needed right now... So, Sammy
said to our son, 'okay, give it a go... We're behind
you...' *(She continues to look through things as:)* He'd
said to me that his newer stuff, poems, were getting so
plain, that it scared him. 'They're becoming like a glass
of water,' he said, something like that. *(Then)* When I
found him on the floor... His eyes were open. I said to
myself, Paula—that's not Sammy...I was so sure that
that wasn't him... He was elsewhere and that's when I
felt a hand on my shoulder. I said, that's him... *(Then)*
'I want to exult.' Those words, a sentence he said to
me one night has stayed with me... And I don't know
what he meant. *(A piece of paper in her hand:)* He had a
superstition—whenever he felt a cold coming on, he'd
write out a poem—always one by Auden—and stick
it his shirt pocket...I guess to ward stuff off... *(Then)*
When he died he had this in his pocket.

(Then)

PAULA: Read it...

NINA: *(Reads)*
"Follow, poet, follow right
To the bottom of the night,
With your unconstraining voice
Still persuade us to rejoice.

"With the farming of a verse
Make a vineyard of the curse,
Sing of human unsuccess
In a rapture of distress;

"In the deserts of the heart
Let the healing fountain start,
In the prison of his days

Teach the free man how to praise."
(Then. Smiles) He told a faculty meeting that Auden
was his favorite Black poet… *(Then)* I know Sammy's
in this house…I can't sell it. I don't want to go
anywhere…I know I'm a good economist. I deserve
this job… Maybe I come from a different time. *(Shrugs)*

PAULA: I'm sure you're a good teacher…

NINA: Maybe… Sammy was. I heard him tell a kid…
Someone had said something to him. He was upset…
And Sammy took the boy aside: your Mother's Black,
your father's white—you're a nation… *(She has opened a
small book, and this stops her.)*

PAULA: What's that… ?

NINA: Read it.

(NINA hands the book to PAULA.)

PAULA: *(Reads)* "He said he likes Sammy's smile. He
said, it was as big as the world." Henry?

NINA: I wrote things down…

PAULA: How old was he then?

NINA: Let me see… *(Then)* About two and a half…

PAULA: *(Another entry in the Baby Book))* "I was doing
the dishes —." This is you.

NINA: Yes. All of this is me.

PAULA: *(Reads)* "The dishes and he said, gesturing
at his right hand, 'no tricks here.' His magic trick…"
(She smiles, looks up, then continues:) "Then he opened
his hand to show it was empty. Then 'no tricks here.'
Gesturing at his left hand, it was empty too. Then he
took two steps over to the cupboard and pulled out the
red kerchief, he'd hidden it on the shelf. His first magic
trick! What a performer!"

NINA: Two and a half.

PAULA: Under baby's favorite toys: 'He loves books!'

NINA: Duh... That boy had no choice...

PAULA: *(Reads)* "He will sit for long periods of time quietly perusing books. Particularly cute when sitting with one heel on the other knee in the little rocking chair..." I bought you that rocking chair.

NINA: You did. That's right...

PAULA: *(Reads)* "looking very grownup and relaxed."

NINA: This is what I do now instead of sleeping... Read through these...

PAULA: "At five weeks old he loves to push up with his legs as I hold him under the arms." "Baby's first steps. Five weeks..."

NINA: I showed the baby book to Samuel, like a year ago... He asked for some reason what I remembered from when Henry was a baby, and I said—don't trust my memory. *(Smiles)* But I have this... *(Then)* He said—he had an idea for a poem. So he was looking for something... I thought I'd show it to Henry's girlfriend...

PAULA: Nice idea... *(Reads)* "Four years old: he chose one of his shells—a small orange spiral shell—from his collection to give to Samuel for his birthday..."

NINA: So this is in October.

PAULA: *(Reads)* "He had been moving it to different hiding spots around the house for several weeks. Its final resting place had been underneath a big hat. He had admonished Sammy not to look—he promised he wouldn't. Finally on the day, we wrapped the shell..."

NINA: He helped.

PAULA: "When Sammy opened it at the Birthday lunch, Henry declared, 'If a robber comes, you can stick it in his eye!'"

(NINA *and* PAULA *laugh.*)

NINA: So it was a practical gift… Here, I'll show you my favorite… (*She turns to a page.*)

PAULA: You read it…

(PAULA *hands* NINA *the book.*)

NINA: (*Reads*) "Sammy has developed a series of classifications for Henry's conduct: there's Good Kid First Class, on down to Good Kid Fourth Class, which is not a *bad* boy, but not terrific. On Wednesday I had to go into the city for a filling, so they were together from nine to four-thirty, the first time I'd been away from both of them for such a long stretch. When I came back, he told me Henry had slipped down to the category of 'kid'."

(*Then*)

PAULA: (*Reads on a small envelope*) "Baby's lock of hair. Age twenty-seven months. First haircut." You want more coffee?

(NINA *nods.* PAULA *will pour more coffee as:*)

NINA: Here's the poet…

PAULA: Sammy?

NINA: No, Henry. (*Reads*) "Walking together to the deli to get the newspaper… he did 'step on a crack, you'll break your mudder's back.' Then began to improvise: 'step on the grass, you'll break your fadder's..' He said, 'you know what I was going to say, Mom?" I paused and said, no Henry, what? He said, 'Glasses'. But it didn't rhyme too well."

(*Laughter*)

(*Now* NINA *is trying not to cry as:*)

NINA: This: "Today he was busy doing things and he passed by me with this comment, 'I'm happy as

nature.'" Where did that come from? Sammy used it in
a poem.

PAULA: Of course he would. Have you ever shown
these to Henry?

NINA: I've tried. Sort of. I'm not sure he's interested.
(As she continues to look through the baby book:) They're
bringing out Sammy's Collected Verse now... *(Then.
Reads:)* "'Wearing his cowboy shirt and vest the other
day, Sammy seeing that Henry wasn't finishing his
lunch, said 'cowboys eat a lot'. Henry answered,
'This cowboy don't...'" *(She takes a deep breath. Then
something catches her eye. She looks off.)*

PAULA: What?

NINA: The sun... Just a sliver... *(Another deep breath)*
We made it. You can go back to bed.

PAULA: I've had two cups of coffee...I'm not going
back to bed, Nina. *(Then)* I told Gretta I'd take her to
Poets' Walk. I've been telling her what a beautiful park
that is...

NINA: Oh, that's a good idea...

PAULA: You want to come?

(No response)

PAULA: I told her it's where we scattered Sammy's...

NINA: I didn't tell you this... And I don't think you
ever saw this. Sammy would always do it... Sometimes
it pissed me off. I'd try to get him to go out, get some
exercise. Get some air. Get away from his goddamn
desk. He'd say, okay, okay, Nina, let's do Poets' Walk.
And then he'd stand and do this very funny, silly walk.
(Laughs) Sort of like... *(As she sits she mimes Sammy's
silly walk.)* You know, because he's a poet...

PAULA: I got it. Very Monty Python.

NINA: Oh right... Yeh. I hadn't thought of that...

PAULA: So will you go with us?

(No response.)

(NINA stands and goes to the CD player on the counter:)

PAULA: You mind if I put…?

NINA: You know I want that CD back… It's mine…

(NINA turns on the Robeson CD. Curly Headed Baby plays.)

(NINA and PAULA listen:)

Oh, my baby, my curly-headed baby,
We'll sit below the sky and sing a song
To the moo-oo-oo-oon.
Oh, my baby, my little darkie baby,
Your daddy's in the cotton field,
Workin' for the fo-oo-oo-oo-od

PAULA: You know, there were people….

NINA: What?

(NINA turns down the music, then:)

PAULA: People who wanted to kill Paul Robeson. String him up on a tree. They did that to an effigy of him. Burned a cross… Where he was supposed to give a concert. He had to hide. This wasn't that far from here, I think…

NINA: I know…Peekskill.

(Then)

PAULA: Why did they do that? *(Then)* Of course, that's a rhetorical question… *('Smiles')*

(NINA turns up the music:)

So, la-la-la-la-la-la lullaby-by.
Does you want the moon to play with?
All the stars to run away with?

They'll come if you you don't cry.
So, la-la-la-la-la-la lullaby-by.

(PAULA *stands.*)

PAULA: I'm going to wake-up my white girlfriend. *(She smiles.)*

NINA: *(A joke)* Isn't she more than that, Paula?

(Then)

PAULA: More than a girlfriend? Yeh. She is.

(Smiles)

NINA: Thanks for keeping me company...

(PAULA *goes.*)

(NINA *listens:*)

In the mammy's arms be creepin',
An' soon you'll be a-sleepin'.
Laa-laa la-la-la-la-la lullaby
Oh, my baby, my curly-headed baby,
I'll dance you fast asleep and love you so
As I si-ii-ii-ii-ing
Oh, my baby, my little darkie baby,
Jus' tuck your head like little bird,
Below its mammy's wi-ii-ii-ii-ing
So, la-la-la-la-la-la lullaby-by
Do you want do moon to play with?
All the stars to run away with?
They'll come if you you don't cry.
So, la-la-la-la-la-la lullaby-by.
In the mammy's arms be creepin',
An' soon you'll be a-sleepin'.
Laa-laa la-la-la-la-la-la lullaby

(Lights fade.)

END OF PLAY

NOTE

The songs sung by Paul Robeson are from *A Lonesome Road,* Academy Sound and Vision Ltd *(1964).*